TOP CLASS

Vocabulary

Year 5

Now supported with CPD training
For info visit www.johnmurraycpd.co.uk

Hopscotch
A division of MA Education Ltd

John Murray

Published by Hopscotch, a division of
MA Education, St Jude's Church,
Dulwich Road, London, SE24 0PB
www.hopscotchbooks.com
020 7738 5454

©2016 MA Education Ltd

Written by John Murray

Series designed by Claire Swaffield,
Fonthill Creative, 01722 717029

Cover illustration by Sara Anderton
www.catandfoxadventures.com

Illustrations by Emma Turner and Sara Anderton

Associate Publisher: Angela Morano Shaw

ISBN 978 1909 860155

All rights reserved. This resource is sold subject to the condition that it shall not, by way of trade or otherwise, be lent, hired out or otherwise circulated without the publisher's prior consent in any form of binding or cover other than that in which it is published and without a similar condition, including this condition, being imposed upon the subsequent purchaser.

No part of this publication may be reproduced, stored in a retrieval system, or transmitted, in any form or by any means, electronic, mechanical, photocopying, recording or otherwise, without the prior permission of the publisher, except where photocopying for educational purposes within the school or other educational establishment that has purchased this book is expressly permitted in the text.

Every effort has been made to trace the owners of copyright of material in this book and the publisher apologises for any inadvertent omissions. Any persons claiming copyright for any material should contact the publisher who will be happy to pay the permission fees agreed between them and who will amend the information in this book on any subsequent reprint.

Cover image of *Melvin McGee: Zombie Hunter* by Mathew Sullivan on page 25, featured by permission of Alan Peat www.thecepress.com

Contents Page

Introduction	6
Word Meaning	8
Word Families	12
Prefixes	16
Suffixes	20
Compound Words	24
Synonyms	28
Homophones	32
Homonyms	36
Homographs	40
Formal English	44
Informal Speech	48
Ye Olde English	52
Foreign Words	56
Creative Word Play	60

Introduction

Top Class is a series that endeavours to combine traditional approaches to the teaching and learning of grammar, punctuation and vocabulary with new techniques and activities that support and encourage good learning.

The three core areas have been separated into three distinct books aimed primarily at Key Stage 2. The three books ought to be used in conjunction with each other in order to provide learners with a wider learning environment and for them to understand that these core elements of Literacy work together and are not to be applied in isolation.

Specific elements of the new Key Stage 3 National Curriculum have also been included in order to introduce Key Stage 2 learners to more complex grammatical constructions and vocabulary as they make their transition from attaining National Standard to Mastery in writing.

Each book, one for each Year group in Key Stage 2, aims to promote discussion about specific areas of Literacy and provide experiences and opportunities to use and apply what they have learnt.

The three books are as follows:

- **Top Class – Grammar**
- **Top Class – Punctuation**
- **Top Class – Vocabulary**

Each book contains lessons that develop a 'top-down' approach, allowing learners to see how we use language in context, not simply *when* we use a particular word, punctuation mark or grammatical construct but *how* to use it to its best effect when writing independently.

As such, it actively promotes the core principle that to learn grammar and punctuation well and to extend your personal vocabulary effectively, then you must not only see these particular elements of Literacy within authentic and meaningful context and settings but you must then have the opportunity to apply what you have understood in your own independent writing.

All too often children are taught grammar, punctuation and vocabulary with exercises that aren't rooted within an authentic experience; and, as a result, although they may gain full marks in their exercise books, they often misapply or omit what has been learnt in their own free writing.

The *Top Class* series seeks to address this problem using a three staged approach, each Lesson Plan being structured so that learners are encouraged to investigate and explore the English language; initially with support and guidance from their teacher and fellow peers before being asked to apply what they have learnt as individuals.

Think about...

Before undertaking the Guided activity, learners are asked about what they already know about a particular piece of punctuation or grammatical form and where they might have seen it.

This links directly to the Guided text, again helping learners to view grammar, punctuation and vocabulary in context, housing it so that stronger links can be made with prior learning and personal experiences. This can then be used as a springboard to explore and develop this further in a familiar setting.

For example, when looking at our use of capital letters when writing a proper noun, learners may be asked about why people use an atlas or map before looking at a tourist map of London and considering why place names and famous tourist attractions start with a capital letter.

Guided

This is a shared activity that engages the whole class.

Set within a specific and relevant genre of Literacy, it embeds each particular piece of grammar, punctuation or vocabulary being taught in a focused and meaningful way. Moreover, it invites learners to use this information in order to answer a series of questions that are related to the text itself and then begins to move beyond it.

Each of the three questions asked have been carefully formatted so that valuable practice for the end of *Key Stage 2 English grammar, punctuation and spelling test* can be undertaken throughout each Year group. Marks are also available so that pupils gain practice at providing fuller explanations for those questions where two or three marks are being awarded. Answers are provided on the Lesson Plan.

Independent

This activity can be completed as an individual, with a partner or within a small group.

Each Independent activity within the book is also differentiated at an upper and lower level* and offers teachers a range of practical activities that support learners as they practice what they have learnt in the Guided section.

*Differentiated activities can be found on the CD Rom.

Homework

Included in this section is a homework activity that aims to encourage wider learning outside of the classroom to take place. There are two types of homework activities that are provided, each having been designed to help learners discover and engage with grammar, punctuation and vocabulary in the 'real' world:

A] Specific 'closed' questions may be asked in order that research skills, both modern and traditional, can be employed to find a particular answer.

For example: What is the capital city of Denmark? Who was the first man to walk on the moon? When necessary, answers are provided on the Lesson Plan.

B] Wider 'open' tasks are given in order to afford learners the opportunity to explore the world around them and collect examples that are both pertinent and authentic.

For example, learners may be asked to find three examples where a shop's name uses an apostrophe in their local high street.

Extension

This final stage of the learning journey is an important one and underscores the importance of using a 'top-down' approach to the teaching and learning of grammar, punctuation and vocabulary.

Each Extension activity within the book is also differentiated at an upper and lower level.*

Its aim is to encourage children to apply what they have learnt in a meaningful and purposeful way in order to embed their learning.

For example, learners may be asked to write a shopping list when planning a party that will naturally include a colon or use strong adjectives to describe a certain event in a story.

More importantly, it is this *writing for purpose* (rather than to score arbitrary marks or achieve irrelevant ticks in an exercise book) that provides a meaningful opportunity for individuals to engage with the English language and create their own work that uses grammar, punctuation and vocabulary in a way that brings their work to life.

In this way, not only will each learner be encouraged to use particular forms of grammar, punctuation or vocabulary correctly but, essentially, they will gain a strong sense of themselves taking an active role as a writer. It gives them a valuable sense of what it is like to be an author, one who uses grammar not only to improve the quality of their work but also to express themselves as best they can using the written word.

The journey from simply understanding how the English language works to being able to apply that knowledge in order to become a capable and confident writer is a journey that will continue into adulthood and one that, in all truthfulness, never really ends.

However, by providing meaningful activities for both the classroom and beyond, the *Top Class* series can help each and every writer to freely use grammar, punctuation and vocabulary to great effect and support them as they endeavour to bring the written word to life in order to inform, influence and entertain their readers.

Differentiated activities can be found on the CD Rom.

TOP CLASS - Vocabulary - Year 5

Word Meaning

Think about...
Who gave you your name?
Why did they choose this name?
What does your name mean?
Where does it originate from?
Is this the same for your surname?

Guided

You are looking at the meaning of names and where they come from.

Focusing upon the meaning of a person's name that resonates with your learners will allow you to explore the derivation of first and last names in a meaningful way, as well as facilitate discussion as to the cultural, historical and personal attachment names often carry.

Once done, answer the questions on page 9.

Independent

You are investigating the history of Britain using maps and place names.

On your own, with a partner or in a small group; complete the task sheet provided to you by your teacher on page 10.

Once finished, cut off the homework task to help you broaden your word knowledge through practical reading within a variety of contexts.

Extension

Extend your personal vocabulary and understanding of specific words. Complete the task sheet on page 11.

If you have one, put any words you find interesting in your Personal Dictionary, together with an example of how it can be used effectively in a sentence.

* Answers available on the CD Rom.

Answers

1 I. To think carefully for a length of time.
II. To give in honour.

2 Allow for personal response

3a secular

3b Christ – <u>Christ</u>ianity is the faith that follows Christ; <u>Christ</u>ians being the people who follow his teachings. It is for this reason that both words begin with a capital letter.

Homework

- No specific answers are required for this homework and learners are to be encouraged to personalise their research in order to present their discoveries to the class.

Two helpful websites are:
www.namedaycalendar.com
www.babynames.net

Remember...
Names are very important. They don't just tell us what a person or place is called but they can hold a cultural, historical and personal meaning too. Names are part of **our heritage** so it is good to understand them fully so that we can treasure them.

Word Meaning

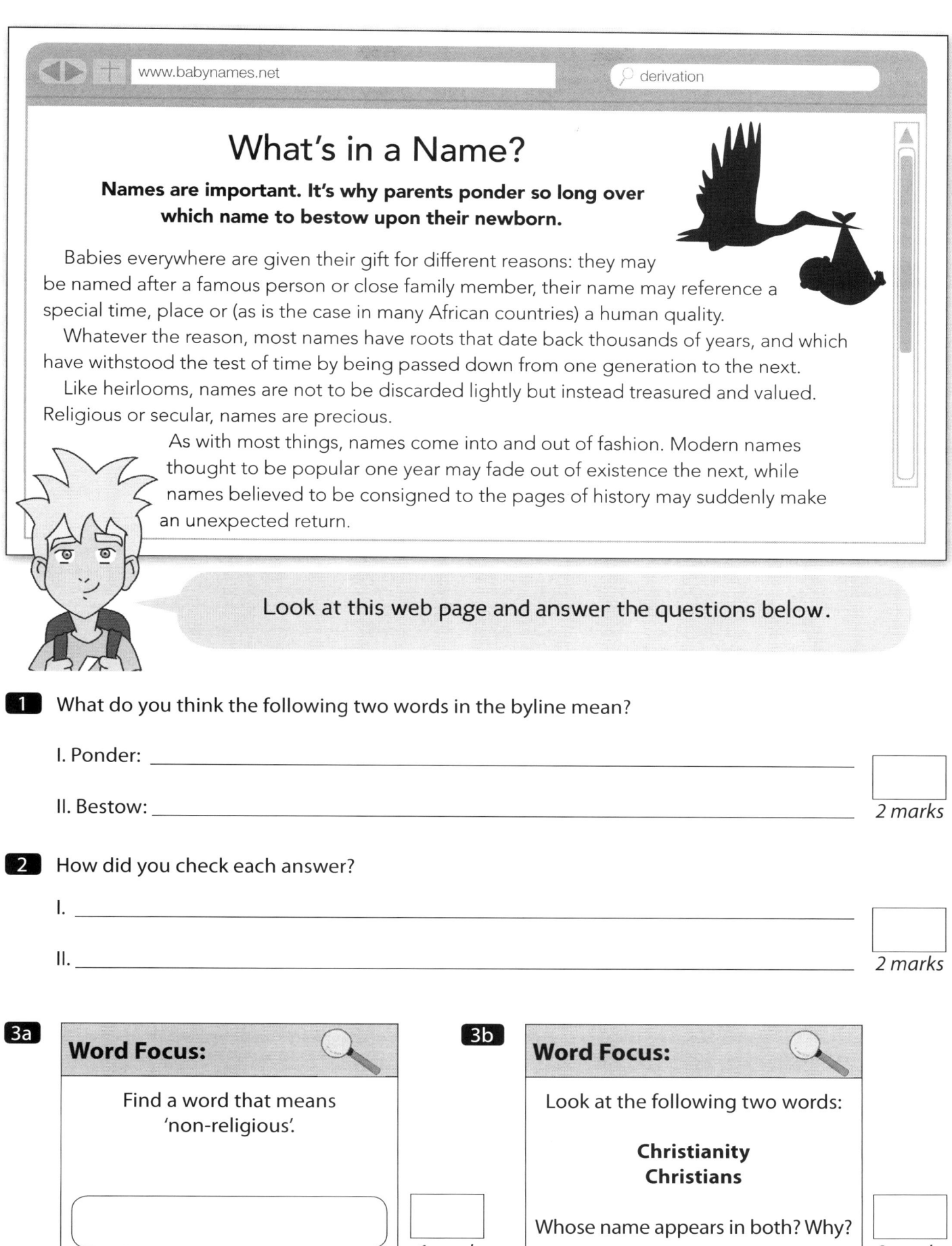

What's in a Name?

Names are important. It's why parents ponder so long over which name to bestow upon their newborn.

Babies everywhere are given their gift for different reasons: they may be named after a famous person or close family member, their name may reference a special time, place or (as is the case in many African countries) a human quality.

Whatever the reason, most names have roots that date back thousands of years, and which have withstood the test of time by being passed down from one generation to the next.

Like heirlooms, names are not to be discarded lightly but instead treasured and valued. Religious or secular, names are precious.

As with most things, names come into and out of fashion. Modern names thought to be popular one year may fade out of existence the next, while names believed to be consigned to the pages of history may suddenly make an unexpected return.

Look at this web page and answer the questions below.

1 What do you think the following two words in the byline mean?

I. Ponder: _____

II. Bestow: _____

2 marks

2 How did you check each answer?

I. _____

II. _____

2 marks

3a Word Focus:
Find a word that means 'non-religious'.

1 mark

3b Word Focus:
Look at the following two words:

Christianity
Christians

Whose name appears in both? Why?

3 marks

TOP CLASS - Vocabulary - Year 5

Word Meaning

How old is the town, city or village where you live? When was it first settled and by who? Look at an Atlas of the UK. Find at least four place names for each example and label the map below.

Place Names:

caster = fort	ton = farm or village
burg/borough = fort	cester = fort
ham = home	by (Danish) = village
kirk = church	stead = large farm
ford = river crossing	chester = fort
beck = stream	dale = valley

Key: Roman   Anglo-Saxon   Viking

What does the place name where you live tell us?

Homework

Look at your personal name.
- Where does your surname come from?
- What does it mean?
- What does it tell you about your family history?
- How is your first name translated in other countries?

Vocabulary

Revisit the text on page 9. Answer each question below.
Highlight the words you explore in the text itself.
Think of ways in which you can learn each one.
Can you act it out or draw it?
Does it remind you of a word you already know? Why?
How will you use your new words in the future?

Name: **Date:**

Find a word that uses the prefix '**pop**'.

What do you think this prefix means?

Which words use this prefix, for the same reason?

population	unpopular
popcorn	pop music
poppy	populate

Shade your answers.

Is the word '**discarded**' positive or negative?

+ −

Why do you think this?

What do you think the word '**discarded**' means?

☐ Thrown away
☐ Kept safely
☐ To be ignored
☐ To be kept in your mind

Which two words do not use the prefix '**dis**'?

disappear	disagree
disco	disarm
disapprove	distance

Are the other words usually positive or negative?

What does the word '**ponder**' mean?

☐ To think for a long time
☐ To think for a short time
☐ To think carefully
☐ To think carelessly

Who is '**heir**' to the throne?

Draw and label your answer.

Underline the root in the word

heirloom

What do you think an heirloom is?

TOP CLASS - Vocabulary - Year 5   11

Word Families

Think about...
Look at the following words:
Inspector spectacles bespectacled respect spectator spectacular spectacle inspect speculate
[Latin] specio = to see or observe
Discuss how these words are related to each other.

Guided

You are about to read an extract from a children's novel entitled *'The Song of a Thousand Dreams'*.

What do you think this song might be about? How might it sound? Where and when might it be sung and by who? Give reasons for your answers and compare them with the answers given by other members of the group you are with.

Once done, answer the questions on page 13.

Independent

You are investigating how different words are related to each other.

On your own, with a partner or in a small group; complete the task sheet provided to you by your teacher on page 14.

Once finished, cut off the homework task to help you broaden your word knowledge through practical reading within a variety of contexts.

Extension

Extend your personal vocabulary and understanding of specific words. Complete the task sheet on page 15.

If you have one, put any words you find interesting in your Personal Dictionary, together with an example of how it can be used effectively in a sentence.

*Answers available on the CD Rom.

Answers

1 Security/secure, pianist/piano, fourteen/fortnight

2 Allow for personal response

3a solo

3b Allow for personal response: 'fort' is short for 'fourteen' and there are 14 nights (2 weeks) in a 'fortnight'.

Homework

- The male – it is a mating song sung to attract females

- The South East: Essex, Suffolk, Norfolk, Kent and Sussex

- A secretive bird best seen April to September

- The birdsong can be heard from April to late May/early June

---

Remember...
When we understand the **root** of a word, then we can begin to understand how different words that use the same root relate to each other. Learning **word families** is a great way to extend your word knowledge and appreciate where words come from.

Word Families

The Song of a Thousand Dreams

Tick...tock...tick...tock... Time dripped by.

Goldie peered through the bars and stared at the framed patch of blue sky in front of her.

A light breeze kissed the flower that had been placed upon the piano. Edith's fingers were too painful to play anymore.

She yearned to be outside; the Thompsons were always popping outside...it must be the most wonderful of places to visit.

She listened to the happy birdsong that drifted over the rose garden and into the lounge. She often sang her own song, much to the delight of Edith and Joe, but her solo rendition was often mistaken as being bright and cheerful.

It had been a fortnight since Joe had left the cage door open but Goldie had been too afraid of the unknown to seize her chance and take flight. Joe had been forgetting to secure the latch more and more of late.

In some ways she would miss the Thompsons but even the smallest of us dream of greater things.

Look at this extract and answer the questions below.

1 Find a word that is most likely to be related to the following:

security [ ]   pianist [ ]   fourteen [ ]

3 marks

2 How do you think each word is related?

I. _____

II. _____

III. _____

3 marks

3a Word Focus:

Which word tells us that Goldie sings her song alone?

1 mark

3b Word Focus:

In your own words, explain how you think the word 'fortnight' was created?

3 marks

Word Families

Look at the word wall. Pair up two related words and colour them the same colour. Underline the root in each word and think about what it could mean. How does this root help you to work out the meaning of each individual family word?

We Are Family!

microphone	photograph	nationality
century	thermometer	In<u>spec</u>tor
prisoner	photosynthesis	cyclone
<u>spec</u>tacular	international	telepathy
recycle	phonics	hypothermia
television	percent	imprisoned

spec = see/observe		

Homework
Read about the nightingale: www.rspb.org.uk
- Is it the male or female nightingale that sings?
- Where in the UK are you likely to see them?
- When are you most likely to see them?
- When are you most likely to hear their song?

Vocabulary

Revisit the text on page 13. Answer each question below.
Highlight the words you explore in the text itself.
Think of ways in which you can learn each one.
Can you act it out or draw it?
Does it remind you of a word you already know? Why?
How will you use your new words in the future?

Name: **Date:**

Find three words that use a suffix meaning '**full of**'.

1. _____

2. _____

3. _____

Underline the root in the word

framed

Draw a window frame.

Draw and colour **Goldie**.

How do you think she got her name?

Draw a '**latch**' on a door.

When you '**seize**' an opportunity, how do you grab it?

☐ Quickly
☐ Slowly
☐ Weakly
☐ With strength

How many nights are in a '**fortnight**'?

What do you think the word '**yearned**' means?

_____
_____

Check your answer in a dictionary.

How strong is a '**light breeze**'?

No wind   *Lots of wind*

| 1 | 2 | 3 | 4 | 5 |

Is there a light breeze outside today?

Prefixes

Think about...
Do you know who Rudyard Kipling is?
Yes: What do you already know about him?
No: How might you find out who he is?
Look at the words: **biology, biography, biodegradable**
How are they related? What does 'bio' mean?

Guided

You are reading an extract from a biography on Rudyard Kipling.

What is a biography? How does it differ from an autobiography? How will this alter the writing style? What do you predict you will read about?

Once done, answer the questions on page 17.

Independent

You are investigating prefixes and their meanings.

On your own, with a partner or in a small group; complete the task sheet provided to you by your teacher on page 18.

Once finished, cut off the homework task to help you broaden your word knowledge through practical reading within a variety of contexts.

Extension

Extend your personal vocabulary and understanding of specific words. Complete the task sheet on page 19.

If you have one, put any words you find interesting in your Personal Dictionary, together with an example of how it can be used effectively in a sentence.

*Answers available on the CD Rom.

Answers

1 Return(ed), remembered

2 Transferred

3a Animation

3b Literacy, literature, literate

Homework

- October 18th, 1967

- $4 million
  (it has since made over $205 million)

- Bruce Reitherman

- Wolfgang Reitherman was his father

Remember...
A **prefix** is found at the start of a word. Many prefixes come from ancient Greek. This is because Greece was once a World Empire and its language, both spoken and written, spread far and wide. If we know what a prefix means it can help us understand what a word means too.

Prefixes

Rudyard Kipling (1865 - 1936)

The first English writer to receive the Nobel Peace Prize for Literature, he is best known for his poems and short stories set in India during the British imperial rule.

Born in Bombay, on December 30th, the first five years of his childhood were spent with his parents. However, at the age of five he was sent back to Sussex, England, to live with foster parents.

It would be a further twelve years before he was to return to his birthplace, this time as a journalist who wrote poetry and fiction in his spare time.

Despite gaining acclaim for his fictional work, including books such as *Plain Tales from the Hills* (1888), his stay in India was not to be a permanent one. After initially moving to Vermont in the States, Kipling eventually settled in his much loved Sussex.

By now he had become an immensely popular writer and poet for both children and adults. *The Just So Stories* (1902) were originally written for his daughter Josephine, who tragically died of pneumonia at the tender age of six. His poem *If* (1895) is often voted the Nation's Favourite. However, it is perhaps *The Jungle Book* (1894) for which he is best remembered, especially after Mowgli's adventures in the Indian jungle were transferred to the big screen in the Disney animation that bore the same name in 1967.

Look at this biographical extract and answer the questions below.

1 Find two words that use the prefix 're' meaning 'again'.

2 marks

2 Which word uses the prefix 'trans' meaning 'to move across'?

1 mark

3a **Word Focus:**
Find a formal word used instead of 'cartoon'.

1 mark

3b **Word Focus:**
The prefix 'lit' means 'letters'. Circle the words below that use this prefix.

**Literacy literature little
litre literate litter**

3 marks

TOP CLASS - Vocabulary - Year 5

Prefixes

Match each definition to a prefix. Underneath each prefix list at least four words that use this prefix.
What does each word mean?
How are these words related?
Use a dictionary to help you.

Prefixes:

trans	**micro**	**inter**	**dem**
(_____)	(_____)	(_____)	(_____)
Examples:	*Examples:*	*Examples:*	*Examples:*

Definitions:

Light   Between   Far   Small   Across   People   Three   Again

re	**photo**	**tri**	**tele**
(_____)	(_____)	(_____)	(_____)
Examples:	*Examples:*	*Examples:*	*Examples:*

Homework

Find out about the 'The Jungle Book' animation of 1967.
* When was the release date?
* How much did it cost to make?
* Who provided the voice of Mowgli?
* How was he related to the director of the film?

Vocabulary

Revisit the text on page 17. Answer each question below. Highlight the words you explore in the text itself. Think of ways in which you can learn each one. Can you act it out or draw it? Does it remind you of a word you already know? Why? How will you use your new words in the future?

Name: | **Date:**

What type of stories would a '**journalist**' write?

☐ Fictional stories for children

☐ Factual news stories for all ages

☐ Narrative poems for adults

Underline the root in the word **tragically**

How sad is this word?

A little sad   *Extremely sad*

1   2   3   4   5

Find a word that means '**to last for a very long time or forever**'.

Put this word in a sentence of your own.

Find a strong synonym that the writer uses instead of '**very**'.

Check your answer in a dictionary.

Draw and label your favourite animated character from a Disney film.

Write the informal word for '**animation**'.

Name your favourite. Draw and label it.

Underline the root in the word

Initially

What are your initials?

What do you think '**initially**' means?

☐ Firstly

☐ Secondly

☐ Finally

Suffixes

Think about...
Look at the following words:
Hopeful   Relentless
Which might you use to describe a battle?
Why? How do they differ?
Which other words might you use? Why?

Guided

You are thinking about remembrance and considering a poem written on the battlefield in WWI.

In which country is Flanders? Find it on a map. Who was fighting who? Why? What weapons were used during this battle? What were the conditions like? Why do you think somebody would write a poem in the pockets of silence on a battlefield rather than wait until they returned home?

Once done, answer the questions on page 21.

Independent

You are investigating derivational suffixes.

On your own, with a partner or in a small group; complete the task sheet provided to you by your teacher on page 22.

Once finished, cut off the homework task to help you broaden your word knowledge through practical reading within a variety of contexts.

Extension

Extend your personal vocabulary and understanding of specific words. Complete the task sheet on page 23.

If you have one, put any words you find interesting in your Personal Dictionary, together with an example of how it can be used effectively in a sentence.

*Answers available on the CD Rom.

Answers

1 Merciless

2 Without mercy – the battle was bloody and violent, it never ceased and did not care who it killed and how.
Allow personal responses to this word picture too.

3a Foe

3b Faithful, faithless
Allow for personal response

Homework

- Western Belgium April 22nd – May 25th, 1915
- Allow for personal research – many will concentrate on the trenches while others may focus on the battlefield itself
- Chemical weapons (chlorine gas)
- Allow for personal response

Remember...
A suffix is found at the end of a word. There are two kinds of suffixes. **Derivational suffixes** help us to create new words from words we already know. If we know what the suffix means, then we will understand what the new word means too.

TOP CLASS - Vocabulary - Year 5

Suffixes

The Second Battle of Ypres was in its infancy; the battle merciless. On May 2nd, 1915 a German artillery shell exploded and a young Canadian, Lieutenant Alexis Helmer, was killed.

That evening, under a blanket of darkness, his close friend, John McCrae, was asked to conduct the burial service - the chaplain had been called away. Later that very night, he sat in deathly silence and began to pen the most enduring poem of World War I.

In Flanders Fields

In Flanders fields the poppies blow
Between the crosses, row on row,
That mark our place; and in the sky
The larks, still bravely singing, fly
Scarce heard amid the guns below.

We are The Dead. Short days ago
We lived, felt dawn, saw sunset glow,
Loved, and were loved, and now we lie
In Flanders fields.

Take up our quarrel with the foe:
To you from failing hands we throw
The torch; be yours to hold it high.
If ye break faith with us who die
We shall not sleep, though poppies grow
In Flanders fields.

Look at the war poem and notes to answer the questions below.

1 Which word uses a suffix that means 'without'?

1 mark

2 What impact does this word choice have upon the reader?

4 marks

3a Word Focus:

Which synonym is used instead of 'enemy'?

1 mark

3b Word Focus:

Find a word in the poem that you can add the two suffixes to:

+ ful   **+less**

Explain how they differ.

3 marks

TOP CLASS - Vocabulary - Year 5

Suffixes

Look at each suffix below. What do you think it means? Use it to create a new word from words given to you. What does each new word mean? How does it relate to the old word? Can you think of an example of your own? Write a definition for each suffix.

Derivational Suffixes:

+less			+ful			+ment			+ship		
worth		power	dread		harm	resent		bereave	friend		hard
↓	↓	↓	↓	↓	↓	↓	↓	↓	↓	↓	↓
1	2	3	1	2	3	1	2	3	1	2	3

+ify			+ible			+able			+ant		
terror		horror	horror		terror	comfort		break	please		defy
↓	↓	↓	↓	↓	↓	↓	↓	↓	↓	↓	↓
1	2	3	1	2	3	1	2	3	1	2	3

+ent			+ ence			+ance			+tious		
absorb		depend	persist		violent	appear		resist	caution		infection
↓	↓	↓	↓	↓	↓	↓	↓	↓	↓	↓	↓
1	2	3	1	2	3	1	2	3	1	2	3

Homework

Reflect upon the Second Battle of Ypres.
- Where and when did this battle take place?
- What were the conditions like?
- Which weapon was used for the first time?
- How do you think the soldiers felt?

Vocabulary

Revisit the text on page 21. Answer each question below.
Highlight the words you explore in the text itself.
Think of ways in which you can learn each one.
Can you act it out or draw it?
Does it remind you of a word you already know? Why?
How will you use your new words in the future?

Name: **Date:**

Find an Old English word for '**enemy**'.

What do you think '**amid**' means? Why?

_____

_____

Check your answer in a dictionary.

What time is '**dawn**'?

☐ Morning
☐ Evening
☐ Sunrise
☐ Sunset

Find a word that means '**an angry disagreement**'.

_____

A little angry   *Extremely angry*

1   2   3   4   5

Why does '**Flanders**' use a capital letter?

_____
_____
_____

How often do you hear something if it is '**scarce**'?

Not a lot   *A lot*

1   2   3   4   5

Put it in a sentence of your own.

Draw and label a '**lark**'.

What does the word '**ye**' mean?

_____

_____

Put it in a sentence of your own.

TOP CLASS - Vocabulary - Year 5

Compound Words

Think about...
Join the following words to 'where':
some   about   else   any   ever   as
What does each new word mean?
What do we call these types of words?
Do any use a hyphen to form a compound phrase?

Guided

You are considering the difference between compound words and phrases.

What do you think the difference is? Why do we sometimes use a hyphen and at other times not? What does a hyphen look like? How is it different to a dash?

A hyphen links two words together to clarify their meaning and creates a compound word or phrase. A dash separates two parts of a sentence when a full stop is too strong but a comma is not strong enough.

Once done, answer the questions on page 25.

Independent

You are creating and comparing compound words and phrases.

On your own, with a partner or in a small group; complete the task sheet provided to you by your teacher on page 26.

Once finished, cut off the homework task to help you broaden your word knowledge through practical reading within a variety of contexts.

Extension

Extend your personal vocabulary and understanding of specific words. Complete the task sheet on page 27.

If you have one, put any words you find interesting in your Personal Dictionary, together with an example of how it can be used effectively in a sentence.

*Answers available on the CD Rom.

Answers

1 Everything, supermarket, birthday

2 Brain-scoffing, zombie-apocalypse

3a lunchtime

3b Allow for personal response: The stress sits firmly on the word 'those' rather than 'days' in order to highlight that this is no ordinary day…and that it is a little bit crazy to say the least! Getting learners to verbalise this phrase will help them hear where the stress lies and understand what it is trying to emphasise.

Homework

- Marek Jagucki

- Over 20 years: across Europe, Asia and North America

- My Big Fat Zombie Goldfish by Mo O'Hara

- The Fintastic Fish-Sitter, The Seaqual, Fins of Fury, Any Fin is Possible

---

Remember...
A **compound word** is created by joining two smaller words together to form a new word. However, sometimes we use a hyphen to link two words together to make a **compound phrase** in order to clarify its meaning.

Compound Words

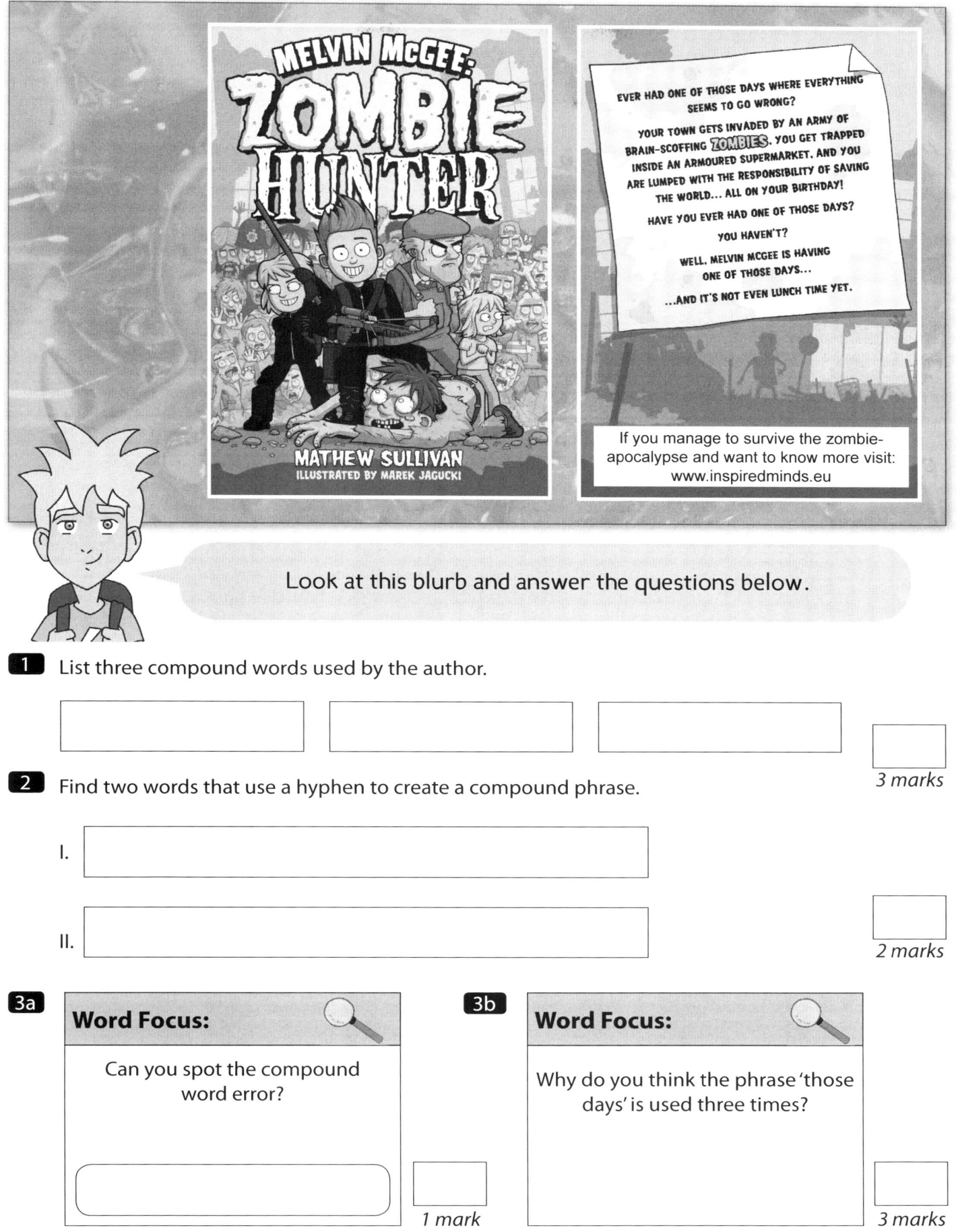

Look at this blurb and answer the questions below.

1 List three compound words used by the author.

[ ] [ ] [ ]

3 marks

2 Find two words that use a hyphen to create a compound phrase.

I. [ ]

II. [ ]

2 marks

3a Word Focus:

Can you spot the compound word error?

[ ]

1 mark

3b Word Focus:

Why do you think the phrase 'those days' is used three times?

3 marks

Compound Words

Sometimes it is easy to make a compound word; we just join two words together. Sometimes it's harder because we need to use a hyphen. Sometimes we even use two hyphens! How crazy is that?
Read the interview and find an example of each type. Why do you think each is used?

An Interview:

Right Mat, what inspires you to write?

My own, more-than-slightly strange brain...usually! Some authors complain about writer's block or the struggle to come up with new ideas, but my problem is rather different. Since I was young, my imagination has run like it's fed on daydream-powered rocket fuel, so the challenge for me comes in sifting, organizing and funnelling all those haphazard ideas into something that will a) excite readers and b) makes at least a morsel of sense. After all, who wants a story that makes complete sense... that'd be boring!

I'm also inspired by the desire to be different - to tell stories that I don't think have been told before. This probably explains my love of comic superheroes: each one unique in their powers, abilities and backstory. It definitely explains why I chose to tell the story of a zombie-apocalypse from the perspective of ten-year-old Zombie Hunter: Melvin McGee!

Homework

Visit www.mjcartoon.co.uk
- What do the initials MJ stand for?
- For how long has he been illustrating?
- Name another zombie book that he has illustrated.
- List four books in this series that are in his portfolio.

Vocabulary

Revisit the text on page 25. Answer each question below.
Highlight the words you explore in the text itself.
Think of ways in which you can learn each one.
Can you act it out or draw it?
Does it remind you of a word you already know? Why?
How will you use your new words in the future?

Name:	**Date:**
Who '**illustrated**' this book? Can you think of two related family words?	How would you describe a '**zombie**'? Draw your answer.
What do you think a '**zombie-apocalypse**' is?	What time is your '**lunchtime**'?
Why might he not have used the word '**dinnertime**'?	When you are '**scoffing**' somebody's brain, how are you eating it? | Fast | Slow | | Neatly | Messily | | Quietly | Noisily | Shade your answers.
What does the word '**armoured**' tell us about the supermarket? Check your answer in a dictionary.	What do you think the word '**lumped**' means? Check your answer in a dictionary.

TOP CLASS - Vocabulary - Year 5

Synonyms

Think about...
Why do pirates scare people?
Is this justified, even today? Discuss.
Look at the following two words:
Glanced   Stared
How are they similar? How are they different?

Guided

You have been asked to write about a flag of your choice for homework. You have decided to research the infamous Jolly Roger.

What do you think this pirate flag looks like? Draw and share your answer. Why have you chosen to draw this design? Where did you get your idea from: a book, a film, a piece of art? Your teacher will now show you a traditional Jolly Roger. How does it compare to yours? Do you know how it got its name?

Once done, answer the questions on page 29.

Independent

Consider how sailors might look upon a pirate flag.

On your own, with a partner or in a small group; complete the task sheet provided to you by your teacher on page 30.

Once finished, cut off the homework task to help you broaden your word knowledge through practical reading within a variety of contexts.

Extension

Extend your personal vocabulary and understanding of specific words. Complete the task sheet on page 31.

If you have one, put any words you find interesting in your Personal Dictionary, together with an example of how it can be used effectively in a sentence.

*Answers available on the CD Rom.

Answers

1 vagabond
   scoundrels

2 Allow for personal response

3a swashbuckling

3b Jolly: happy and smiling
   Grin: a wide, often open, smile

Homework

- No specific answers are required for this homework, though learners could be encouraged to present their work as a Power Point presentation to the class.

Lessons on how to use Power Point to make presentations more interesting can be undertaken during ICT in order to embed these skills further.

Remember...
A **synonym** is a word that has a similar meaning to another. However, there are no true synonyms in the English language. Every word has its own unique meaning. We must understand the shades of meaning a word has if we are to use it correctly and to its greatest effect.

Synonyms

In times gone by the sight of a Jolly Rodger would strike fear into the hearts of all who looked upon it. But where did this peculiar name originate? After all, 'jolly' isn't the first word that springs to mind when you think of swashbuckling pirates and 'Roger' is a rather pleasant name if you ask me.

The most plausible explanation is that it comes from the English word "Roger" meaning "wandering vagabond". So frowned upon were these scoundrels that they even referred to the Devil himself as "Old Roger" during this period. The depiction of a devil being placed upon a pirate flag was not uncommon.

The second theory is that it derives from the 17th century French phrase "jolie rouge" meaning "pretty red". Not all pirate flags were black and white; many included red because of its terrifying association with blood.

The least likely idea comes from the fact that Asian pirates gave their captains the title "Ali Raja", meaning "King of the Sea". Some believe that it is possible that the English adapted this term over time, 'Jolly' simply referring to the apparent grin of the skull itself.

Look at this Fact File and answer the questions below.

1 Find a negative word that the writer uses instead of...
Draw a skull next to the most negative word.

| Pirate: | Pirates: |

2 marks

2 On a scale of 1-5, how strong is the word 'pleasant'?

Weak   1   2   3   4   5   **Strong**

Can you think of a stronger synonym the writer could have used? Use a thesaurus.

4 marks

3a Word Focus:
Which word means 'fighting in a brave, exciting and courageous way'?

1 mark

3b Word Focus:
What is the difference between being 'jolly' and having a 'grin'?

3 marks

TOP CLASS - Vocabulary - Year 5

Synonyms

Look at these synonyms that describe how someone might look upon an object. How do they look at it? Is it quick or slow, for a long or short period of time? Colour in your answers. How is your character feeling? Make notes beside your answer.

Key Word: glare – glares - glared

Definition: to give a long, fixed angry look, usually wide-eyed and with raised eyebrows.
Example: Mr Smith glared at Tom, his eyes telling him to shut up…right now!

	How did they look at the object?				How is the character feeling?
glared	fast	slow	long	short	Mr Smith is glaring at Tom as he wants him to be quiet but can't use his voice.
gazed	fast	slow	long	short	
glanced	fast	slow	long	short	
stared	fast	slow	long	short	
browsed	fast	slow	long	short	
glimpsed	fast	slow	long	short	
examined	fast	slow	long	short	

Homework

Read about a famous historical pirate.
- When did they live and how did they die?
- What was the name of their ship?
- What was the design of their pirate's flag?
- Why did they design it to look like this?

Vocabulary

Revisit the text on page 29. Answer each question below.
Highlight the words you explore in the text itself.
Think of ways in which you can learn each one.
Can you act it out or draw it?
Does it remind you of a word you already know? Why?
How will you use your new words in the future?

Name: **Date:**

Find a word which means '**very odd**' or '**strange**'.

Put it in a sentence of your own.

Find a formal word meaning '**believable**'.

Put it in a sentence of your own.

Underline the root in the word

frowned

Draw a pirate with a frown on his face.

Find a formal word the writer uses instead of '**changed**'.

Put it in a sentence of your own.

Draw and label a '**skull**'.

What is this made from?

Why does the term '**Jolly Roger**' start with capital letters?

Find a formal word that means '**comes from**'.

Put it in a sentence of your own.

Underline the root in the word

depiction

What do you think this word means?

TOP CLASS - Vocabulary - Year 5

Homophones

Think about...
Correct this sentence:
Your to old two play inn the sandpit.
What was wrong? Why?
What might have caused the errors?
What do we call these types of words?

Guided

You're looking at a friend's email that he is about to send to his pen pal.

What is a pen pal? What does this term suggest about where Jo lives? What else in the email suggests Jo does not live near to Harry? Will Harry's email be formal or informal? Why? What might you expect to read in Harry's email? What would you write about if your pen pal was about to visit you?

Once done, answer the questions on page 33.

Independent

Consider how some words that sound the same but are spelt differently possess different meanings.

On your own, with a partner or in a small group; complete the task sheet provided to you by your teacher on page 34.

Once finished, cut off the homework task to help you broaden your word knowledge through practical reading within a variety of contexts.

Extension

Extend your personal vocabulary and understanding of specific words. Complete the task sheet on page 35.

If you have one, put any words you find interesting in your Personal Dictionary, together with an example of how it can be used effectively in a sentence

*Answers available on the CD Rom.

Answers

1 I, you're, It's, raining, here, know, your, inn

2 to, see, new, night, ate, too, through, not

3a cheers

3b there – it refers to a place or location

Homework

- No specific answers are required for this homework, though teachers should ensure that the correct format, style and language choices are used when writing an informal email to a friend.

Remember...
A **homophone** is a word that sounds the same as another but is spelt differently and has a different meaning.

Homophones

Inbox (1)
Drafts
Sent
Spam
Trash

To: jo@talktalk.net
CC:
Subject: **RE: Hi Their Jo**

Aye hope your OK. Its reigning hear in Manchester, despite it being summer! I don't no why we don't have webbed feet and quack, lol. Bring you're waterproofs and a dinghy just inn case.

I went too sea the knew Star Wars film last knight. It was awesome! It was a bit dear but well worth it. I eight far to much popcorn threw it though, knot to mention the foot long hotdog b4 it had even started.

Anyway, bee gr8 2 c u next weekend, whatever the whether. Dad is gonna take us camping and teach us to cook on an open fire…can't weight. Mum said two tell ewe wheel pick you up from the airport.

Cheers big ears,

Harry

Look at this email and answer the questions below.

1 List the eight corrections needed in paragraph one.

4 marks

2 List the eight corrections needed for paragraph two.

4 marks

3a **Word Focus:**
Find the informal word Harry uses instead of 'thanks'.

1 mark

3b **Word Focus:**
Which word should Harry have used in the Subject box?
Their   They're   There

Why?

3 marks

TOP CLASS - Vocabulary - Year 5

Homophones

Cut out the homophones below. Shuffle them and place them face down. Take turns with a partner to choose two cards. If they are a matching homophone keep them and play again. If not, turn them back over. The winner will have the most cards at the end.

Sounds Good to Me!

weather	you're	new	through	cheque
sew	bored	its	knew	their
flower	tail	peace	seen	piece
leak	sow	threw	tale	flour
leek	shore	they're	your	it's
check	scene	whether	board	sure

Homework

Send a classmate an email.
- Introduce yourself in a light-hearted way.
- Tell them about something you did last weekend.
- Suggest something you could both do together.
- Invite them round and then close.

Vocabulary

Revisit the text on page 33. Answer each question below.
Highlight the words you explore in the text itself.
Think of ways in which you can learn each one.
Can you act it out or draw it?
Does it remind you of a word you already know? Why?
How will you use your new words in the future?

Name:	Date:
Draw and label a '**dinghy**'.	Draw and label a duck's '**webbed**' feet.
Draw and label the two compound words in paragraph two. How are they linked?	List the four compound words found in paragraph three. |	
--	--	 Put them in a sentence of your own.
Find an American synonym for '**rubbish**'.	Find the informal word Harry uses instead of '**Thanks**'. When else might you hear this word?
Draw and label an '**open fire**'.	Is a '**spam**' email usually positive or negative? (+) (-) Why?

TOP CLASS - Vocabulary - Year 5

Homonyms

Think about...
What do you already know of King Arthur?
Make a list with your teacher.
Look at the following words:
Castle   Knight
What does each word mean as A] a noun B] a verb?

Guided

You are reading a modern retelling of a classic - the legend of King Arthur.

How did he become King? What did he have to do? What was inscribed upon the stone? Did he know straight away that he had fulfilled the prophecy? Why do you think he was able to pull the sword from the stone when no other could?

Once done, answer the questions on page 37.

Independent

You are investigating homonyms.

On your own, with a partner or in a small group; complete the task sheet provided to you by your teacher on page 38.

Once finished, cut off the homework task to help you broaden your word knowledge through practical reading within a variety of contexts.

Extension

Extend your personal vocabulary and understanding of specific words. Complete the task sheet on page 39.

If you have one, put any words you find interesting in your Personal Dictionary, together with an example of how it can be used effectively in a sentence.

*Answers available on the CD Rom.

Answers

1 [Verb] Sink: To a lower level
[Noun] Sink: A bowl attached to a wall

2 [Verb] To sink: to fall

3a The hilt

3b pinballing – This creative word play establishes that this is a modern retelling of the Arthurian legend, pinball machines being popular in the mid 20th century. It offers the reader an image of a boy lost going from one tree to another, quickly and in desperation in the hope he will eventually find his escape.

Homework

- Camelot
- Queen Guinevere
- Sir Lancelot
- Merlin

Remember...
A **homonym** is a word that sounds the same and is spelt the same as another but has a different meaning.

Homonyms

Whoso pullet out this sword from this stone is rightfully King of England born.

The moon gazed upon the boy pinballing his way through the old wood.

'How can I find a sword for Kay when I can't even find my own way back home?' he huffed.

Suddenly, the trees released him and he stepped into the clearing. A sleeping church loomed above him. The boy's heart sank.

Just then, a glint of moonlight caught his eye.

Could this really be? A sword set within a stone? If he could only set it free, then Kay would be able to compete in the tournament after all!

He laid his hands upon the hilt and closed his eyes...

'For my brother,' he whispered.

The sword shone as it was released from its stony internment and was held aloft.

The boy scuttled down the path, his heart rejoicing in the belief that his quest was now over.

Little did he know that this was only a beginning. The prophecy had come true; England had just witnessed the anointing of its new king...a boy called Arthur: pure of heart and noble in deed.

Look at the Arthurian legend and answer the questions below.

1 How is the present tense for the word 'sank' a homonym?

_____

_____ *2 marks*

2 Explain how someone's heart can 'sink'. Use a dictionary to help you.

_____

_____ *2 marks*

3a **Word Focus:**
What do we call the handle of a sword?
Draw it.

1 mark

3b **Word Focus:**
Find the word 'pinballing'.
Why do you think the writer has chosen to create this new word?

3 marks

TOP CLASS - Vocabulary - Year 5

Homonyms

Look up each homonym in a dictionary.
How does each example differ in meaning?
How would you classify each one?
Can you put each word in a sentence to illustrate how they are different?
Which homonyms might you associate with castles?

Long Live the King!

wood	clearing	bow	beams
bat			flags
knight			rocks
dust			iron

1. _____
2. _____
3. _____
4. _____
5. _____
6. _____
7. _____
8. _____
9. _____
10. _____

Homework

Read about King Arthur.
- In which castle did Arthur reside?
- To whom did he get married?
- Which knight betrayed him?
- Which mysterious magician helped him?

Vocabulary

Revisit the text on page 37. Answer each question below.
Highlight the words you explore in the text itself.
Think of ways in which you can learn each one.
Can you act it out or draw it?
Does it remind you of a word you already know? Why?
How will you use your new words in the future?

Name: **Date:**

What do you think the word '**pullet**' means? Act it out.

_____

_____

What does it tell us about the spelling of words?

Draw the '**hilt**' of a sword.

Add a '**glint**' of moonlight to it.

Underline the root in the word

clearing

Draw a clearing in the old wood.

A '**quest**' is a journey that is…

Quick	Difficult
Easy	Long
Focused	Aimless

Shade your answers.

Look up the word '**loomed**'.
What does it tell us about the church?

_____

_____

_____

How does Arthur feel when he '**huffed**'.

_____

_____

Act it out.

Find a French word for a '**competition**'.

Arthur '**scuttled**' down the path.

Quickly	Slowly
With long strides	With small steps

Shade your answers. Act it out.

TOP CLASS - Vocabulary - Year 5

Homographs

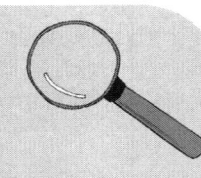

Think about...
Which superhero lives in Gotham City?
List some villains he has to defeat.
Do you know who the Riddler is?
Underline the root word in his name.
What is a riddle? Do you know any?

Guided

You are looking at the Police File on the Riddler.

What is a riddle? Why do you think they are so popular? Your teacher will now give you a riddle the Riddler has left behind for you to solve. Can you work out what the answer is before it's too late? Be quick…the clock is ticking!

Once done, answer the questions on page 41.

Independent

You are the Riddler and have set a friend some riddles to solve!

On your own, with a partner or in a small group; complete the task sheet provided to you by your teacher on page 42.

Once finished, cut off the homework task to help you broaden your word knowledge through practical reading within a variety of contexts.

Extension

Extend your personal vocabulary and understanding of specific words. Complete the task sheet on page 43.

If you have one, put any words you find interesting in your Personal Dictionary, together with an example of how it can be used effectively in a sentence.

*Answers available on the CD Rom.

Answers

1 minute (unit of time), minute (very small)

2 dove (bird), dove (simple past of 'dive')

3a penchant

3b puzzles, conundrums, riddles

Answers to the riddles on page 42: wound, bow, moped, tear, lead, close, research, content, refuse and entrance

Homework

- Bob Kane (1939)
- Wayne Manor, a huge mansion on the outskirts of Gotham City, USA.
- Robin (Timothy Drake), Alfred
- Allow for personal response

Remember...
A **homograph** is a word that looks like another because it is spelt the same way. However, when we say each word out loud we say it in a different way. This is because we put the **stress** in each of the two words in a different place. Sometimes it goes up and sometimes it goes down.

Homographs

Police File: Edward Nigma

Name: Edward Nigma (AKA The Riddler)

DOB: October 1st, 1948

Location: Gotham City

Edward Nigma is no ordinary criminal mastermind. With his superior intellect and obsession with creating clever conundrums and perplexing puzzles, this enigmatic enigma is one of the Dark Knight's most fearsome foes.

You may recognise him from his alter ego...The Riddler!

A scrawny fellow with a penchant for green and purple, his brilliance is underlined by his lack of empathy - he often uses innocent civilians as bait; using them as disposable pawns in a battle of wits.

With his passion for posing puzzles and ever-more elaborate riddles to solve, it is hardly surprising that his crimes have inevitably led to him being a semi-permanent resident of the infamous Arkham Asylum.

Look at the Police File and answer the questions below.

1 Riddle me this! What do we call a very small unit of time?

2 marks

2 Riddle me this! Which bird jumped into water head first yesterday?

2 marks

3a **Word Focus:**
Find a French word that means 'to have a liking for, especially something that others might not'.

1 mark

3b **Word Focus:**
List three synonyms used instead of the word 'problems'.

3 marks

Homographs

The Riddler sends you a cryptic note.
It reads:
A puzzle, a quandary, a riddle you see,
But can you work out what the answer should be?
Try to work out each riddle.
Why do you think you have solved it?

Riddle Me This!

I am a deep cut on a toy soldier.	I am a polite weapon.	I am what a sulking teenager would ride.
I am the ripping of watery sadness.	I am a heavy metal dog walker.	I am near enough to shut this.
	I am a scientific study, looked for again.	I am happy with all that is in there.

Homework
Visit www.capstonekids.com/characters
* Who created the character of Batman?
* Where does Batman live?
* Who is Batman's A) sidekick B) butler
* Create a Police File on one of Batman's foes.

Vocabulary

Revisit the text on page 41. Answer each question below.
Highlight the words you explore in the text itself.
Think of ways in which you can learn each one.
Can you act it out or draw it?
Does it remind you of a word you already know? Why?
How will you use your new words in the future?

Name: **Date:**

What do the letters **AKA** stand for?

A -

K -

A -

Is the word '**infamous**' positive or negative?

(+)   (-)

Why do you think this?

_____

Find two phrases that use alliteration in paragraph one that mean '**very puzzling**'.

I. _____

II. _____

If you '**lack empathy**' how much of it do you have?

None   *Plenty*

1   2   3   4   5

If you are '**scrawny**', how do you look?

☐ Fat
☐ Thin
☐ Healthy
☐ Unhealthy

(+)   (-)

Underline the root in the word

superior

What do you think this word means?

_____

Look at the Riddler's name:
E.Nigma

What do you notice?

_____

What do you think the word '**enigmatic**' means?

_____

_____

Check your answer in a dictionary.

Formal English

Think about...
Look at the following names:
Tim   Timmy   Timothy   Timo
How are they the same? How do they differ?
Which is the most formal? When would you use it?
Can we say and write other names like this? Discuss.

Guided

You are remembering THE GREATEST COOK in the world... Vera Worthington!

How good a cook do you think she was? Where do you think she cooked and for who? What do you think she would look like? Draw your answer. What might have been her most famous dish? What might it have been well known for?

Once done, answer the questions on page 45.

Independent

You are comparing the formality of words and phrases.

On your own, with a partner or in a small group; complete the task sheet provided to you by your teacher on page 46.

Once finished, cut off the homework task to help you broaden your word knowledge through practical reading within a variety of contexts.

Extension

Extend your personal vocabulary and understanding of specific words. Complete the task sheet on page 47.

If you have one, put any words you find interesting in your Personal Dictionary, together with an example of how it can be used effectively in a sentence.

*Answers available on the CD Rom.

Answers

1 St. Margaret's Primary School
St. Maggie's

2 St. Joseph's, St. Patrick's

3a viper

3b Yes – xxx represent three kisses. It shows Vera was well loved, as does the use of 'Our Vera'. Even though the plaque is serious and respectful, this shows a genuine warmth and affection for a much loved member of the school.

Homework

- The specific answers required for this homework usually appear on a school's website. However, if this is not the case then discussion should take place as to where learners may find this information and how best it may be incorporated in the site in the future.

Remember...
Formal language tends to be cold and serious. We often use it when we don't know the person directly or the situation is serious. **Informal language** is more relaxed. We often use it with when talking about friends or family because it is warm and friendly.

Formal English

> **Our Vera**
> Not the greatest cook in the world but THE GREATEST COOK in the world!
> It was our privilege to have known you. xxx

Her rice pudding was infamous; her custard notorious.
The spark of a rumour once ignited that both were being sought after by the British Army.
Her onion and cheese pie was renowned for its delicate flavours of onion, more onion and (if you were especially lucky) a morsel of extra strong Lancashire cheese. Always served with a generous side order of heartburn, it never failed to amaze all who attempted to eat it.
But what she lacked in culinary skills, she more than made up for in simply being the most loving person you would ever hope to meet.
With a face as fat as butter, purple hair and a tattooed viper wrapped around her neck, Vera Worthington was a sight to behold.
A greasy list of everyone's birthday clung to the canteen wall and, what can only be best described as a 'rock bun', would be made for each lucky recipient. Why? For the same reason she gave Bobby Higgins a lift into school every morning in her sidecar…not because he found it hard to walk or because she had been asked to do so but because "it's always nice to do nice things."
We learnt lots of things at St. Maggie's but it was Vera who taught us the most important things. She fed our stomachs and nurtured our hearts.

Look at this remembrance and answer the questions below.

1 What was the name of the school Vera worked at? Write it formally and informally.

Formal: _____

Informal: _____

2 marks

2 How would you write each of the following two school names formally?

St. Joey's: _____

St. Pat's: _____

2 marks

3a **Word Focus:**
Find a word used for 'a small poisonous snake'.

1 mark

3b **Word Focus:**
Was it right to put 'xxx' on this plaque?

☐ Yes

☐ No

Give reasons for your answer.

3 marks

TOP CLASS - Vocabulary - Year 5

Formal English

Often formal words are longer than informal words. They are usually French or Latin in origin rather than their informal Anglo-Saxon relatives.
Match the formal and informal words together.
When and where might you see each word?
How and why might it be used?

Word Wall:

stop	aroma	wrong	children	get	assistant
require	retain	fix	television	free	bought
photograph	obtain	got	boring	photo	helper
allowed	release	tedious	smell	enquire	purchased
ask	cease	kids	keep	consider	incorrect
think	need	received	permitted	TV	repair

Homework

Read about the history of your own school.
- How did your school get its name?
- In which year was it built?
- What was the name of its first Head Teacher?
- How many pupils first attended the school?

Vocabulary

Revisit the text on page 45. Answer each question below.
Highlight the words you explore in the text itself.
Think of ways in which you can learn each one.
Can you act it out or draw it?
Does it remind you of a word you already know? Why?
How will you use your new words in the future?

Name: **Date:**

Are the words '**infamous**' and '**notorious**' positive or negative?

(+)   (-)

What do they tell us about Vera's cooking?

What do you think the phrase '**lacked culinary skills**' means?

Why do you think the pie is called '**onion and cheese**' and not '**cheese and onion**'?

How large is a '**morsel**' of food?

Tiny   Huge
  1   2   3   4   5

Draw and label your answer.

How hard was the birthday list stuck to the kitchen wall?

Not very   Very
  1   2   3   4   5

Which word tells us this?

Draw a '**viper**' tattoo.

Find a positive word the writer uses instead of '**famous**'

Put it in a sentence of your own.

Find the formal word used instead of '**kitchen**'.

Why do you think the writer chose this word?

TOP CLASS - Vocabulary - Year 5   47

Informal Speech

Think about...
Look at the following invitations:
Anniversary   Birthday Party   BBQ
Wedding   Parents Evening   School Trip   Bike Ride
Put them in order of formality.
Which invites would be spoken and which written? Why?

Guided

You are considering when it is appropriate to use text speech and when it is not.

Think back to the activity you have just completed. Why would it be OK to use a text message on some occasions and not others? What is the difference? How important do you think this is? Why? How might a person feel if you were to invite them to a formal event via a text message? Why?

Once done, answer the questions on page 49.

Independent

You are looking at how informal speech is sometimes represented in text messages.

On your own, with a partner or in a small group; complete the task sheet provided to you by your teacher on page 50.

Once finished, cut off the homework task to help you broaden your word knowledge through practical reading within a variety of contexts.

Extension

Extend your personal vocabulary and understanding of specific words. Complete the task sheet on page 51.

If you have one, put any words you find interesting in your Personal Dictionary, together with an example of how it can be used effectively in a sentence.

*Answers available on the CD Rom.

Answers

1 The informal text abbreviations are as follows:
r, l8r, Sat, avin, c, m8, phn, @

2 BBQ, Y6, info

3a asap

3b wanna – want to
gonna – going to

Homework

- No specific answers are required for this homework, though teachers may wish to take this opportunity to talk about e-safety and discuss the wider implications of owning a mobile phone in a sensitive but proactive manner that is in accordance with Whole School Policy.

Remember...
We **abbreviate** words and phrases in many different ways, especially when texting. However, it is important that we do not use **informal speech** (in spoken or written form) for formal occasions. We must learn when it is appropriate to use text speak and when it is not.

Informal Speech

Dear Parent/Guardian,

You are kindly invited to attend the annual St. Thomas' Barbecue this coming Saturday at twelve noon to help raise funds for the PTA.

Refreshments will be available and our Year Six pupils will be performing as part of our Summer Festival. We request that no photographs or videos be taken during this event and that mobile telephones are switched off during the performance itself.

A donation of £1 per adult is suggested.

Should you require any further information, please do not hesitate to ask.

Yours sincerely,
Mr P. Jameson

P. Jameson

Text message:

Hi m8, we r avin a BBQ on Sat. U wanna come? Pete is gonna b there! It's at 12 @ mine. Txt or phn me asap. Cheers. C u l8r 👍

Look at these invitations and answer the questions below.

1 How are the following words in the text message written informally?

| are | | Saturday | | see | | telephone | |
| later | | having | | mate | | at | |

4 marks

2 How might you abbreviate the following formal words as a text message?

barbecue   Year Six   information

3 marks

3a **Word Focus:**
How is the phrase 'as soon as possible' abbreviated?

1 mark

3b **Word Focus:**
Which two nonsense words should really be spoken and not written?

How would you write each one formally?

3 marks

TOP CLASS - Vocabulary - Year 5

Informal Speech

Look at each text message.
Colour the informal words yellow.
Then write out each text message formally.
Colour the corresponding formal words blue.
Who might have sent each message? Why?
How would you reply?

Txt Talk! 👍

Informal	Formal
Gr8 2 c u – will av 2 catch up soon.	
I'm goin 2 J's l8r. U wanna come 2?	
I avn't got A's numba soz.	
Hi m8, wuu2 @ wkend?	
Dad, cud u do me a fava pls?	
Liz, ope ure gud. Phn me 2nite.	
I'm gonna txt b4 settin off.	
Av gotta go. Sch tomoz!	

Homework

Consider the following statement:
Primary school children should not own a mobile phone.
- List three reasons for this statement.
- List three reasons against this statement.
- What do you think personally? Why?

Vocabulary

Revisit the text on page 49. Answer each question below.
Highlight the words you explore in the text itself.
Think of ways in which you can learn each one.
Can you act it out or draw it?
Does it remind you of a word you already know? Why?
How will you use your new words in the future?

Name: **Date:**

Underline the root in the word

Guardian

Where might you see this protector?

What is the difference between a '**parent**' and a '**guardian**'?

How often does an '**annual**' event occur?

☐ Once a term
☐ Once a month
☐ Once a year
☐ Once in a lifetime

Find a formal word for '**ask**'.

Put it in a sentence of your own.

Why do you think the word '**donation**' is used and not '**fee**'?

Draw and label some '**refreshments**' you may see at the BBQ.

Underline the root in this word.

What does the abbreviation '**PTA**' stand for?

P -

T -

A -

What does the abbreviation '**asap**' mean?

a -

s -

a -

p -

TOP CLASS - Vocabulary - Year 5

Ye Olde English

Think about...
What is a prayer?
When do people say prayers?
Why do people say prayers?
Have you heard the Lord's Prayer?
Should prayers be learnt or spoken from the heart?

Guided

You are considering the Lord's Prayer.

How old is this prayer? When was this prayer first told? Who taught us this prayer? In which language would it have been spoken? Why? What was Jesus trying to teach his listeners? Why do you think this model prayer, above all others, has lasted so long and is said so much in the Christian faith?

Once done, answer the questions on page 53.

Independent

You are an archaeologist and need to translate Old English words into Modern English.

On your own, with a partner or in a small group; complete the task sheet provided to you by your teacher on page 54.

Once finished, cut off the homework task to help you broaden your word knowledge through practical reading within a variety of contexts.

Extension

Extend your personal vocabulary and understanding of specific words. Complete the task sheet on page 55.

If you have one, put any words you find interesting in your Personal Dictionary, together with an example of how it can be used effectively in a sentence.

*Answers available on the CD Rom.

Answers

1 art: is, thy: your, thine: yours

2 Trespasses, trespass*

3a kingdom

3b Hebrew – Literally meaning 'so be it' it is an affirmation of the prayerful words which have preceded it. Its use is found in both the Old and New Testaments, the former being written in Hebrew, the latter predominantly in Greek.

Note: To trespass in times gone by was to break a moral or religious law rather than a criminal act against the law of the land.

Homework

- Spathiphyllum cochlearispathum
- Gustav Wallis (1824)
- The jungles of Columbia
- Yes: it is mildly toxic if ingested

Remember...
All languages change over time. Many centuries ago, people used **Old English** words that we no longer use. However, from time to time, we may come across such words. It is important that we try and understand where these words have come from and what they mean.

Ye Olde English

Look at the Lord's Prayer and answer the questions below.

1 What do you think the following three Old English words mean?

art: _____   thy: _____   thine: _____

3 mark

2 Look at the sign below. Find two family words in the prayer. How are they related?

| Trespassers will be prosecuted |

I. _____

II. _____

2 marks

3a Word Focus:

Which word means 'King's domain'?

1 mark

3b Word Focus:

Do you think the word 'Amen' has a Hebrew or Greek origin?

3 marks

Ye Olde English

You are an archaeologist and discover a bundle of scripts in an old castle. Translate the Old English words into Modern English using modern tools such as a printed dictionary or the Internet to help you.
Match each word up using a different colour.

Old English:

besmirch, ditty, lea, thwart, whence, dint, aye, soothsayer, hither, ye, nay, quench, betroth, brine, oft, thy

Tanslation:

To satisfy a thirst	To stop or prevent a plan or action	Yes	Many times
To be given in marriage	A blow struck by a sword or weapon	A field or meadow	No
Your(s)	A short, simple song	You or the	A person who predicts the future
From that place	A strong salt-water solution used for pickling	To stain or make dirty	Here, to this place

Homework

Read about the Peace Lily plant.
- What is the Latin name for this plant?
- Who first brought this plant to Europe? When?
- Where was this plant discovered?
- Is this well-loved house plant poisonous?

Vocabulary

Revisit the text on page 53. Answer each question below.
Highlight the words you explore in the text itself.
Think of ways in which you can learn each one.
Can you act it out or draw it?
Does it remind you of a word you already know? Why?
How will you use your new words in the future?

Name: **Date:**

Why do the following words use a capital letter? **Heaven Kingdom Earth**	Why do these two words use a capital letter? **Father Name**
Find a word that means '**every day**'. Put it in a sentence of your own.	What does the word '**art**' mean in this prayer? ☐ Painting, drawing or sculpting ☐ Not science ☐ An Old English word for 'is' or 'are'
What does the Old English word '**thy**' mean? Check your answer in a dictionary.	What can the Old English word '**thine**' mean? Check your answer in a dictionary.
What does the word '**hallowed**' mean? ☐ Holy or sacred ☐ Unholy or not sacred	'**Amen**' is an old Hebrew word. Who uses this language today?

TOP CLASS - Vocabulary - Year 5

Foreign Words

Think about...
Look at these two facts:
1. Britain has been conquered many times.
2. Britain was once a World Empire.
List some examples to prove both statements.
What effect will this have had upon our language?

Guided

You are learning about the infamous Battle of Hasting of 1066.

Task: Give a copy of the story on page 57 to pairs or small groups of learners. Ask them to place it in the correct chronological order and take turns retelling it to a partner. Does it make sense? Why did you put it in this particular order? Which key words and clues helped you make your decisions?

Once done, answer the questions on page 57.

Independent

You have become French for the day...c'est la vie!

On your own, with a partner or in a small group; complete the task sheet provided to you by your teacher on page 58.

Once finished, cut off the homework task to help you broaden your word knowledge through practical reading within a variety of contexts.

Extension

Extend your personal vocabulary and understanding of specific words. Complete the task sheet on page 59.

If you have one, put any words you find interesting in your Personal Dictionary, together with an example of how it can be used effectively in a sentence.

*Answers available on the CD Rom.

> Teacher's Note: Animated versions of the Bayeux Tapestry (which includes the correct answers to the Task) are freely available on YouTube and can be used by learners to self-check their answers.

Answers

1 banquet

2 From the Old French 'banc' meaning 'bench'. In medieval times people sat on benches to eat together during celebrations.

3a livid

3b victor: the person who is victorious

Homework

- 70 metres (231 feet) long
- The Museum of Queen Matilda, in the city of Bayeux, Normandy, France.
- Latin – the main written language of the Middle Ages.
- Halley's Comet – A periodic comet that returns to Earth's vicinity around every 75 years, it was seen as a bad omen for Harold and his men.

Remember...
Britain has been **conquered** many times over the centuries and was once a **World Empire**. English is rich because it comes from lots of different places. English is part of our heritage, so we should know where it comes from and how it has grown over time.

Foreign Words

The Battle of Hastings – 1066

Harold sends messengers to France, proclaiming his kingship. ○	The battle rages for hours. William rallies his troops for one last charge. ○	It is October 14th. Battle commences! The Normans outflank the Anglo-Saxons. ○
Loaded with supplies, William and his men set sail across the channel…the Norman invasion has begun! ○	The year is 1066. Harold has not long been crowned King of England, despite his oath to William. ○	After landing at Hastings on the South East coast of England, a banquet is prepared in his honour. ○
A comet is seen during his coronation, an omen that no good will befall England's new monarch. ○	William is livid at Harold's betrayal and orders an invasion fleet to be built. ○	The Normans are victorious and William is crowned King of England on Christmas Day, 1066. ○
	King Harold dies. Legend has it that he is shot in the eye with an arrow. ○	Following the feast, homes are cleared to make way for battle defences. ○

Look at this historical narrative and answer the questions below.

1 Find a French word that means 'a large formal meal for lots of people'.

1 mark

2 This comes from an Old French word meaning 'bench'. How do you think it got its name?

2 marks

3a **Word Focus:** Find a word that means 'extremely angry'.

1 mark

3b **Word Focus:** Underline the root in the word

victorious

What do both words mean?

3 marks

TOP CLASS - Vocabulary - Year 5

Foreign Words

Find each French word listed below in the word search. Once found, put it in a sentence of your own to show that you understand what it means. Think of different ways that will help you spell these words correctly in the future. Don't forget to use the French accent when necessary.

Parlez Vous Francais?

e	t	t	e	l	e	m	o	è	r	s	w	é	r
t	p	é	c	n	a	i	f	d	e	f	t	l	e
t	f	é	w	i	h	r	m	x	s	i	e	è	s
t	m	y	f	q	j	a	n	w	t	c	u	g	e
u	o	p	g	a	f	g	k	b	a	u	q	t	r
o	u	è	e	g	c	e	e	d	u	p	u	j	v
h	s	f	n	i	d	u	h	y	r	é	o	q	o
l	s	l	r	c	k	h	c	c	a	j	b	n	i
i	e	q	e	s	m	k	è	b	n	s	i	h	r
s	o	u	v	e	n	i	r	d	t	u	b	e	d
b	a	l	l	e	t	g	c	u	l	n	y	è	p
é	f	x	w	b	r	u	n	e	t	t	e	t	k

1. ballet
2. souvenir
3. omelette
4. mirage
5. brunette
6. genre
7. café
8. mousse
9. chef
10. bouquet
11. reservoir
12. silhouette
13. restaurant
14. debut
15. fiancé
16. crèche

Homework

Read about the Bayeux Tapestry.
- How long does it measure?
- Where is it kept today?
- Which language appears on the tapestry?
- Which comet appears on the tapestry?

Vocabulary

Revisit the text on page 57. Answer each question below.
Highlight the words you explore in the text itself.
Think of ways in which you can learn each one.
Can you act it out or draw it?
Does it remind you of a word you already know? Why?
How will you use your new words in the future?

Name: **Date:**

What do we call the ceremony whereby a person is crowned King or Queen? Check your answer in a dictionary.	Find a formal word for a '**promise**'. Check your answer in a dictionary.
Find a synonym the writer uses instead of '**angry**'. How angry is it? Quite — 1 2 3 4 5 — Extremely angry	Find another '**angry**' synonym the writer uses to describe the battle. Why do you think this word is used?
Find a formal word the writer uses instead of '**starts**'. Put it in a sentence of your own.	Find an alternative word the writer uses instead of '**King**'. Put it in a sentence of your own.
Is the word '**omen**' positive or negative? (+) (−) What kind of luck did it bring King Harold?	Is a '**banquet**' a formal or informal meal? | Formal | Informal | Colour your answer.

Creative Word Play

Think about...
Your teacher will show you some colours.
What pops into your head with each one?
The final colour is hot pink.
What's the first thing that pops into your head now?
Who might like this colour and who might not? Why?

Guided

Henry Pickles enters the school library to shelter from the rain while he waits for his dad to pick him up in their new family car. There's just one problem…it's hot pink!

What genre of text do you think this story will be? Why? Do you think the fact that it is dad who is driving the car makes the situation funnier or does it not matter? What do you think Henry's reaction will be when he finds out the colour of the new family car?

Once done, answer the questions on page 61.

Independent

Liam and Lucy Lockhart enter the Laughter Library.

On your own, with a partner or in a small group; complete the task sheet provided to you by your teacher on page 62.

Once finished, cut off the homework task to help you broaden your word knowledge through practical reading within a variety of contexts.

Extension

Extend your personal vocabulary and understanding of specific words. Complete the task sheet on page 63.

If you have one, put any words you find interesting in your Personal Dictionary, together with an example of how it can be used effectively in a sentence.

*Answers available on the CD Rom.

Answers

1 The author's name is a pun; it plays on the words "I've (got) a clue"

2 Shhhhhh, tut, honk

3a Allow for personal response

3b **PINK!** The use of capitals and an exclamation mark shows us Henry's loud vocalised shock, which contrasts sharply with the peace and quiet of the library setting.

…that. The italics here emphasises the stress, as does the use of a comedic pause (by means of an ellipsis) that leads into the punch line.

Homework

- This ongoing class project can be placed in the library area for ease of reference and should include headlines, jokes and other examples that use puns in an amusing and clever way.

Remember...
A **pun** is a word or phrase that has more than one meaning or sounds very similar to another word. Playing with spelling can create a good pun and they are often used in memorable headlines or titles for comedic effect.

Creative Word Play

'PINK!' Henry blurted out, despite being the only person standing in the Romance section.

'Shhhhhh,' said Mrs Threadbare. Her eyes bored deep into Henry Pickles' soul and firmly pressed the mute button.

Henry skulked into the Crime section and began thumbing through the pages of a Whodunit: Death in Paradise by Ivor Clew.

'How apt,' he thought. The one shred of street cred he had left after rescuing Twinkles was about to come to an untimely end.

'What if anyone sees me getting into a pink car? What if Sally Grimshaw sees me getting into a pink car?' Life was unbearable.

'I'd rather get soaked,' he grimaced and picked up his bag.

But it was too late; two honk honks announced dad's arrival. Mrs Threadbare let out a tut (though ever so quietly) and she peered through the window in search of another button to press, though which button it was this time was hard to guess.

It was at this very same moment, and much to Henry's horror, that Sally Grimshaw (yes...*that* Sally Grimshaw) walked into the library with none other than Bradley Winterbottom (and before you ask, yes...*that* Bradley Winterbottom).

Look at this comedy and answer the questions below.

1 Why is the book Henry picks up funny?

_____

_____

1 marks

2 Find three onomatopoeic words hidden in this scene. Act each one out.

[ ]   [ ]   [ ]

3 marks

3a **Word Focus:**

Which name do you find the funniest? Why?

1 mark

3b **Word Focus:**

How does the writer show the reader that he wants the following two words stressed?

PINK!   ...that

3 marks

TOP CLASS - Vocabulary - Year 5

Creative Word Play

The books in the Laughter Library are all funny. Whether that's funny ha ha or funny odd is up to you. Match each author and title. Design its front cover. Create two new books for the library. Choose a title and author for each new book.

Puns:

Reaching into his pocket, Liam pulls out half a pencil (chewed at one end of course), a shrivelled up conker (minus the shoelace but an ex-champion nevertheless) and two small coins amounting to the grand total of three pence; oh yes, and his sister's library card.

Book Titles:	Authors:
The Golden Wedding	Mandy Llifeboats
Weekend Breaks	Rosa Cabbages
Shipwrecked!	Percy Vere
Training Wild Cats	Robin D. Banks
Keep Trying	Rufus Blownoff
The Hurricane	Anne E. Versary
Grow Your Own Veg	Gladis Friday
Make Money Fast	Claude Face

Homework

Create a class pun scrap book.
- Where did you find your pun?
- Which newspaper headline or advert used it?
- How did it make you laugh?
- Why is this pun so clever?

Vocabulary

Revisit the text on page 61. Answer each question below.
Highlight the words you explore in the text itself.
Think of ways in which you can learn each one.
Can you act it out or draw it?
Does it remind you of a word you already know? Why?
How will you use your new words in the future?

Name:	Date:

If you '**blurted out**' an answer how would you do it? Act it out.

Quickly	Slowly
Quietly	Loudly
With thought	With no thought

Shade your answers.

What does the word '**bored**' mean in paragraph two?

☐ Not interested

☐ To make a deep hole

How wet is the word '**soaked**'?

Damp   *Saturated*

   1   2   3   4   5

What does tell us about the weather?

Draw the symbol of the '**mute**' button on a remote control.

◯

What does it do?

Is the word '**grimaced**' positive or negative?

    ⊕   ⊖

How are you feeling? Act it out.

Underline the root in the following word

thumbing

What do you think it means? Act it out.

How much is a '**shred**'?

A little   *A lot*

   1   2   3   4   5

Put it in a sentence of your own.

What type of book do you think a '**Whodunit**' is?

Draw and label your answer.

Notes: